First published in paperback in 2003
Published by
Evans Brothers Limited
2A Portman Mansions
Chiltern Street
London W1U 6NR

First published 1999
Reprinted 2001, 2003
© in the text Keith Good 1999
© in the illustrations Evans Brothers Limited 1999

Series editor: Su Swallow
Illustrations and page design: Tim Scrivens, T J Graphics
Production: Jenny Mulvanny

Printed in Hong Kong by Wing King Tong Co. Ltd

Good, Keith
Super Structures. – (Design challenge)
1. Structural engineering – Juvenile Literature 2. Structural
design – Juvenile Literature
I. Title II. Scrivens, Tim
624.1'771

ISBN 0 237 52540 2

For details of initial teacher training and in-service courses in
Design Technology at the University of Greenwich, contact
Keith Good by fax +44 (0)208 331 9504 or e-mail
k.w.good@gre.ac.uk

Acknowledgments

For permission to reproduce copyright material the authors
and publishers gratefully acknowledge the following:

page 6 Last Resort Picture Library **page 8** Last Resort
Picture Library **page 10** Last Resort Picture Library
page 14 Robert Harding Picture Library **page 16** Sylvain
Grandadam, Tony Stone Images **page 20** John Miller, Robert
Harding Picture Library **page 22** Doug Mindell, Tony Stone
Images **page 24** Last Resort Picture Library (the authors
and publishers would like to thank Ragged Bears Publishing
for permission to reproduce this photograph © Paul
Strickland) **page 26** Last Resort Picture Library
page 28 Last Resort Picture Library

DESIGN CHALLENGE

Super Structures

Keith Good

Evans

About this book

About this series

This series involves children in designing and making their own working technology projects, using readily available salvaged or cheap materials. Each project is based on a 'recipe' that promotes success and crucially, stimulates the reader's own ideas. The 'recipes' also provide a good introduction to important technology in everyday life. The projects can be developed to different levels of sophistication according to the reader's ability and can reflect their other interests. The series teaches skills and knowledge in a fun way and encourages creative, innovative ideas.

About this book

Understanding structures matters because they are such an important part of our world. Our skeletons are natural structures, so are shells, spiders' webs and plant stems. People design and make a huge variety of structures to live in, sit on, walk over, carry things or rely on in other ways. Despite their variety, all structures have to be able to stand up to the forces and loads that they will encounter. Through design projects in this book, children discover that some shapes are much stronger than others and how this can save resources. Practical activities in this book give an understanding of structures and how materials behave when different forces act on them. This relates to the Science curriculum e.g. 'compare everyday materials....relate these properties to everyday uses' and 'forces'. Designing stable structures that don't fall over, balancing forces to keep things up and the main kinds of bridges are also covered through activities. Structures that are rigid but can collapse when we want them to (like baby buggies) are important in everyday life and this idea is used as a basis for several design projects. Well designed structures use materials economically. A packaging project raises this issue and encourages wise use of materials. As in every book in this series, the reader is encouraged to get real understanding through marrying 'recipes' and knowledge with their own ideas and imagination.

Safety

● A small screwdriver or awl can be used to make holes but the corrugated card must be supported by a slab of modelling clay or thick card – not a hand. Protect work surfaces with a piece of board.

● If a structure is to be tested to destruction (until it gives way), make it from weak materials like the ones suggested in this book, otherwise dangerous amounts of weight may be needed.

● Adult use of craft knives is strongly advised. These must be used with a cutting board (or mat) and a safety rule with a groove to protect the fingers. Card is often best cut for children on a paper trimmer with a guarded wheel cutter.

Contents

Materials and forces
Testing the strength of materials

All designers (including you) need to choose the right materials for their projects. This means knowing about different forces and how materials behave. Structures have to cope with *static* forces like their own weight and *dynamic* forces like wind. When standing on scales you cause a static force. When you jump on the scales you cause a bigger dynamic force. If we know what kinds of force will work on a structure it helps us to choose materials that will cope. Paper is very strong when pulled (*tension*) but very weak when twisted (*torsion*). Stone and brick are strongest when being squashed (*compression*) but will not bend without breaking. Try these experiments to find out how some materials behave.

You will need

- strips of paper
- thin card
- 30cm plastic ruler
- twig or used match
- elastic band
- modelling clay
- string
- piece of fabric

Bending

1. Take a twig or used match and watch closely as you bend it until it breaks. What happened to the top surface? What happened to the bottom surface?

2. Hold a strip of paper tightly on each side of a plastic ruler. Bend the ruler upwards then downwards. Notice when the strips stretch and squash.

3. Put cuts into both sides of a block of modelling clay and bend it. Which surface is stretched (in tension) and which surface is squashed (in compression)?

1

twig

2

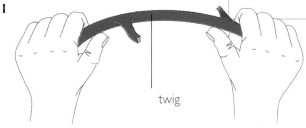

paper

30cm plastic ruler

3

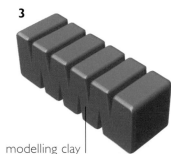

modelling clay

Twisting

Try twisting a strip of paper, modelling clay, string or fabric. Notice how each material behaves.

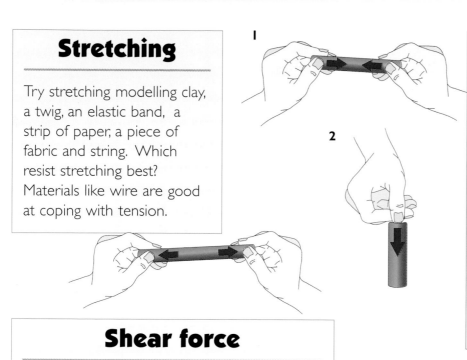

Stretching

Try stretching modelling clay, a twig, an elastic band, a strip of paper, a piece of fabric and string. Which resist stretching best? Materials like wire are good at coping with tension.

Squashing

1. Take a twig and push inwards from each end. Is a short twig stiffer than a long one of the same thickness? How do a strip of paper and piece of string or fabric behave?

2. Make a cylinder of modelling clay and compress (squash) it. It is not brittle and won't break but watch closely how it behaves.

Shear force

Shear forces try to make one part of a structure slide past another.

Shearing happens when scissors cut paper or cloth.

1. Use a hole punch, paper strip and a modelling clay pin to see a shearing force at work. Metal bolts often have to cope with shear forces.

2. Compare paper strips joined by a paper fastener with strips that have been glued and left to dry. Which is best at coping with a pull?

Making holes for bolts and other fixings can cause weakness – this is why many aircraft parts are just glued!

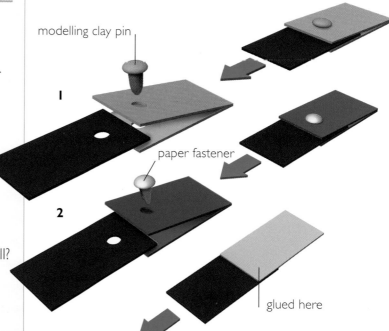

modelling clay pin

paper fastener

glued here

Getting ideas

Design a way to record what happens when you try the activities on these pages. Drawings, charts, lists and perhaps a computer could help you to show your results. Can you collect other materials to try? Make a poster showing bad or silly uses for different materials, like using cheese to make a ladder, polystyrene for a tightrope or string to push something. You could collect and display different materials and pictures of them in use. Think about why different products use different materials. You could separate natural materials like wood and wool from ones made by people, like plastic.

Beams
Making strong shapes

Lots of things that you see every day are shaped to make them strong. Careful shaping saves weight and money, and avoids wasting material. Some food tins and sandwich packaging have ridges to make them strong. Why do you think baby buggies are made from tubes instead of solid bars?

A piece of material that has to resist bending is called a beam. The shape of a beam affects how stiff it is and the load it can carry. Here is a chance to find out about beams for yourself.

Some beam shapes to try

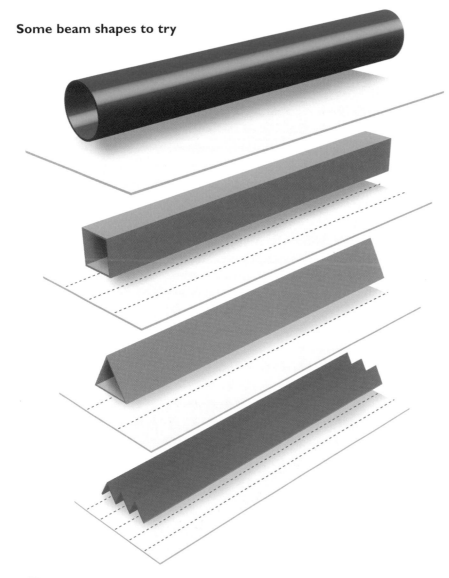

You will need

- Some pieces of A4 paper (use scrap paper if you can) cut in half lengthways
- Sticky tape (masking tape is best)
- Weights e.g. standard metal ones, plasticine blocks of the same weight or a bag of marbles
- 2 piles of books or another way of making a gap for testing your beams

Tip
A worn out ball-point pen, and a ruler are useful for making creases.

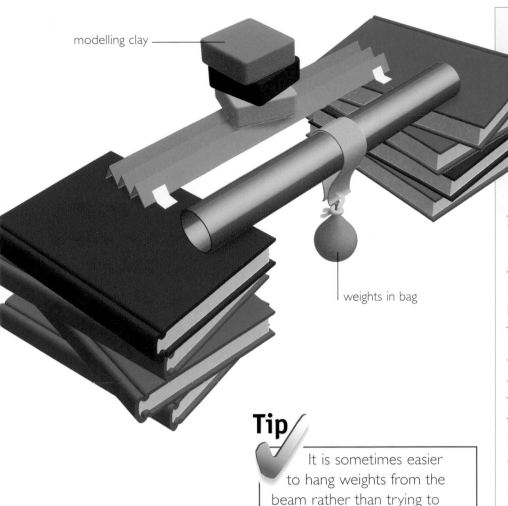

modelling clay

weights in bag

What to do

1. Make the beams shown on page 8, using sticky tape to hold the beams in shape.

2. Arrange your books with a gap of 22cm so that you can test your beams.

3. Try bridging the gap with a flat piece of paper first. Next, test the beams you have made, using enough tape to hold them in shape.

4. Add weight to the middle of your beam a little at a time. **Safety**: don't use weights that are easily broken or heavy and dangerous!

5. Record the shape of each beam and the weight it carried before collapsing.

Tip

It is sometimes easier to hang weights from the beam rather than trying to balance them on top.

Getting ideas

Try out your own beam ideas. Could you combine some of the shapes to make a new idea? Remember, always start with the same sized paper for a fair test.

Can you think of other ways to support a beam?

Look for strong shapes in buildings, sports and play equipment and many other things around you. You could record these with notes and drawings.

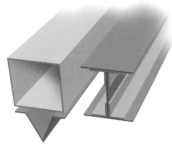

Strong shapes
Triangles and shells

There are two main kinds of structure. Frame structures are made up from pieces which are joined together. Triangles are rigid shapes so they are often used to make strong but light frames. You can see triangles at work in building-site cranes, bridges, bicycle frames and kites. Shell or *monocoque* structures allow thin material to be made much more rigid by forming it into 'shells'. Seashells, eggs and beetle wing covers are examples in the natural world. Domes, egg boxes, plastic bowls, polystyrene food trays and clear plastic bubble packs are examples of shell structures made by people. Try making the shapes on these pages and test their strength.

You will need

- strips of corrugated cardboard (the 'tubes' in the cardboard should run *along* the strips)
- paper fasteners
- 6 sticks or pieces of wooden dowel rod about 30cm long
- elastic bands
- white glue
- clear plastic bubble pack

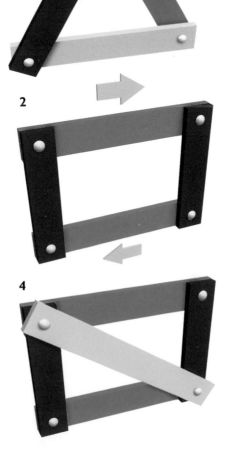

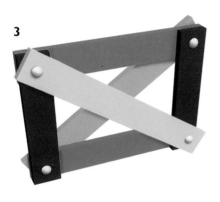

What to do

1. Make a triangular frame using paper fasteners and strips of corrugated cardboard. Notice how rigid the triangle is.

2. Make a rectangular frame and notice how easily it collapses.

3. Now fix two strips across the frame. This is called *triangulation*. Notice how rigid the structure has become.

4. Remove one of the cross pieces and notice that the frame is still rigid. Part of a structure that can be taken away without weakening it is called a *redundant member*.

5. Ask a friend to help you make a *tetrahedron* from sticks and elastic bands (see right). Feel how sturdy it is.

6. Make this bracket from paper fasteners and strips of corrugated cardboard. Stick with white glue. The tubes inside the strips must run along them.

7. Press gently on the bracket and notice how strong it feels.

tetrahedron

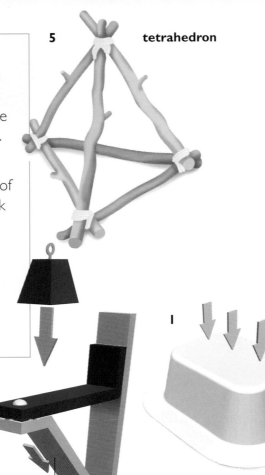

5

6

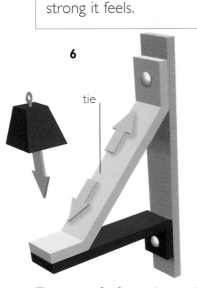

tie

strut

The parts of a frame that are being compressed (squashed) are called struts. Parts that are stretched are called ties.

A triangle makes this bracket rigid. The strut becomes a tie when the bracket is turned upside down.

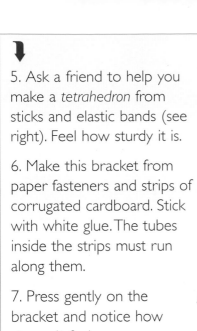

1

2

What to do

Bubble packs are strong shell structures. The shape makes the pack much stronger than a flat sheet.

1. Cup your hand over a bubble pack and press down steadily to feel how strong the structure is.

2. Cut off the flat base to see if this makes any difference to the strength.

To make a special shell structure, see page 20.

Getting ideas

Think of uses for your tetrahedron. Could it be a shelter, a model of play equipment or something else? Could a number of these structures be put together to do useful jobs?

Design uses for the bracket you have made. You could make one or two more and use them to support a small shelf. Make the shelf from corrugated cardboard, taking care that tubes inside run *along* the shelf.

Collect clear bubble pack shell structures. Can you recycle them as the covers for hand-held games that you design? Small balls or cut-out shapes could be steered or tapped into parts of the playing surface. The clear shell lets players see but stops them touching the pieces.

Stable structures
Testing shapes on a test ramp

It is often very important that structures don't tip over in use. A *stable* structure does not tip over easily. An *unstable* structure will tip over easily. People are not very stable structures. When you stand and lean forwards a little you can feel how unstable you are.

The activities here will help you to understand why some things fall over more easily than others. This knowledge should help you design your own stable structures.

You will need

- corrugated cardboard
- A4 card
- paper
- masking tape or clear tape
- modelling clay
- drinking straws
- small cardboard box or tube
- cork
- 2 kebab sticks

What to do

How to make a test ramp. You can share this with one or more friends.

1. Cut a piece of A4 card in half and join the pieces at the end with tape to make a hinge.

2. Stick a strip of corrugated cardboard across the ramp.

3. Fix some paper to a piece of cardboard. Use modelling clay to make some of the shapes shown.

4. Put your shapes against the strip of card and tilt the ramp very slowly. On the paper, mark the angle when the shapes topple. Number the shapes and angle lines.

5. Design your own stable and unstable shapes and try them on your ramp. You could also try other things that won't break.

Do you notice anything about the most stable shapes? Do the least stable shapes have anything in common?

Work out a way to record your results. Show at what angle each shape fell. You could use a computer to help you show your results.

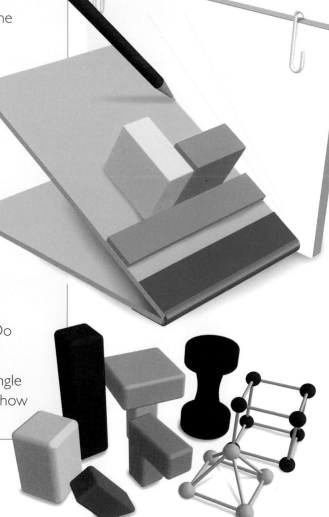

What to do

You might think you can tell how stable a shape is by the way it looks – but you can't always.

1. Tape a modelling clay weight near the top of a small cardboard box or tube. What else could you use as a weight?

2. Try the box or tube on your test ramp. First put the weight at the top, then put it at the bottom. Which way up is the most stable?

Look at cantilevers on page 14.

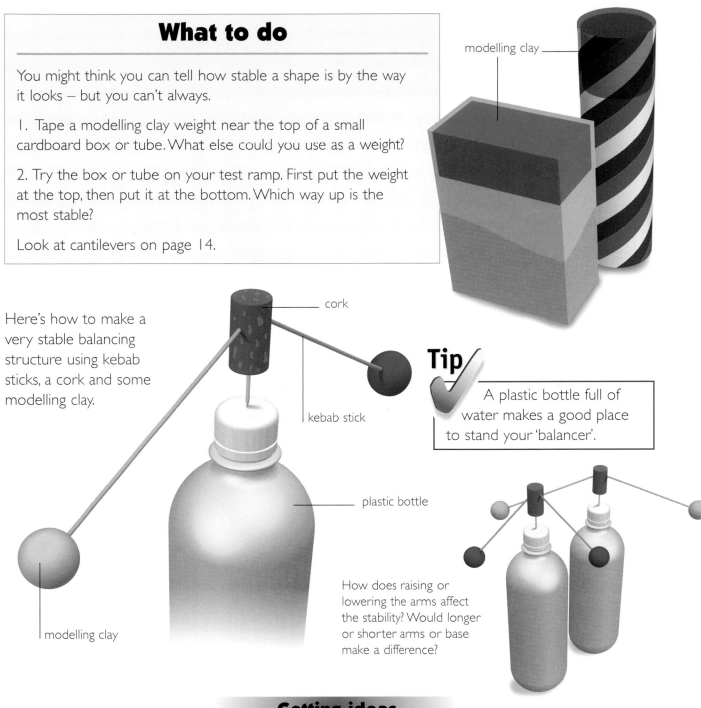

modelling clay

cork

Here's how to make a very stable balancing structure using kebab sticks, a cork and some modelling clay.

kebab stick

Tip

A plastic bottle full of water makes a good place to stand your 'balancer'.

plastic bottle

modelling clay

How does raising or lowering the arms affect the stability? Would longer or shorter arms or base make a difference?

Getting ideas

Make design drawings for a very stable vehicle that would be difficult to turn over. Make design drawings for a new kind of wheeled vehicle to carry a baby and shopping. Could your design carry a toddler too? **Important**: think about where the weight will go so that your design would not tip over. You could model your designs, using a construction kit or other materials and clay weights.

Balancer Try using your stable balancer as part of a design for a game. Could you balance things on the balancer? You could word-process a set of rules.

Equilibrium
Balancing forces to keep things up

When two tug-of-war teams pull with the same amount of force they stay still because their pulling forces *balance* or are *in equilibrium*. If two people of the same weight sit on the ends of a see-saw it will balance. Balanced pulling (tension) from different directions can be used to keep things in place. Radio masts, sailing ship masts, metal chimneys and tents are all held up by balancing the pull of cables or ropes.

Here are some ideas for making structures by balancing forces or getting them in equilibrium. If the forces don't balance, your structures will fall!

You will need

- 30cm ruler
- modelling clay (or small weights)
- rectangular wooden blocks
- paper kitchen towels
- thread
- drinking straw or kebab sticks
- masking tape
- corrugated cardboard
- sheet of A4 paper

What to do

1. Balance a ruler over the edge of a table. Put modelling clay or another small weight on the table end.

2. Put the same amount of weight on the unsupported end of the ruler. How far out can the ruler extend (stick out) without the structure falling?

3. Try adding extra weights to the table end. Each time you add a weight, see how much further the ruler can extend.

How far can a structure that is balanced in the middle be built out on each side? Structures like this are based on balanced cantilevers – a cantilever is a beam that sticks out from its support. Experiment, using toy wooden blocks.

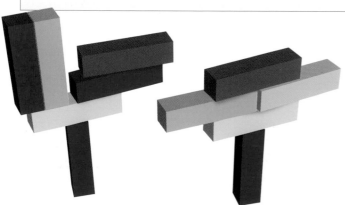

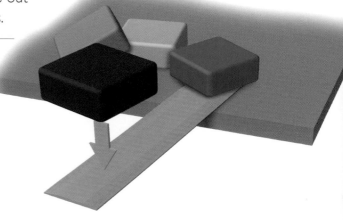

Making a mast

Using only one sheet of A4 paper, and a small amount of masking tape, see how tall a radio mast you can build.

1. Make a base for your mast from a piece of corrugated cardboard.

2. Make stiff shapes from the paper to build your mast (see page 8).

3. Use ties or guy ropes made from thread and fixed with tape to help you support a really tall mast.

Making a tent

Balance the pulling forces on the guy ropes to support tents and shelters.

1. Make a base for your tent from a piece of corrugated cardboard.

2. Try making a tent like the one shown. Use kitchen towel, and straws or kebab sticks, thread and tape. Make the tent as sturdy as possible.

Getting ideas

Tent structures are used as shelters when fishing or camping, and to keep the sun off. They can also be used to protect explorers and to house people after a disaster. Structures like this are easy to fold down into a small space and are quite light to move about. Design and make your own tent structures. You could design a structure with more than one 'room'. Your structure could be for a special purpose. Think about other structures that could be held up by balanced forces. Could you design a hammock supported by poles and ropes? Look in catalogues to see what other people have designed.

Bridges
Bridging gaps with strength and stability

Bridges are important structures. They make journeys shorter, safer and easier. Bridges have to be light so that they do not sag under their own weight or waste materials and resources. They have to be as strong as possible so that they can carry heavy loads. There are four basic kinds of bridge: beam, cantilever, arch and suspension bridge. Find out about bridges by making these.

Beam bridges

Beam bridges can be single span (one beam) or multi-span (several beams).

Frameworks called trusses are often used to make bridges that are strong but light.

thin card

paper triangles

The deck of the bridge rests on top of the framework base

plan

6 cm

6 cm

You will need

- paper artstraws or dried spaghetti
- thin card and paper
- modelling clay
- corrugated cardboard
- string
- masking tape
  - heavy books

What to do

Make your own bridges using artstraws or sphaghetti to bridge a 20cm gap, perhaps between a pile of books.

1. Draw the plan on this page full size and build your bridge sides on it. Hold parts still with masking tape while you glue the paper triangles.

2. Turn the frame over carefully and glue triangles on the other side.

3. Let the sides of your bridge dry before joining them to each other. Don't use too much glue and let it dry well. Glue on a thin card deck (like a roadway) to hold the load.

4. Add a little weight at a time to see how much your bridge can carry. Try different designs and compare yours with others made by friends.

Here are other truss designs. Design your own too. Make full-sized plans.

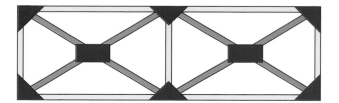

Cantilever bridges

Cantilever bridges are made up of beams that are only supported at one end. Trap one end of a ruler between heavy books to make a quick cantilever. Often two cantilevers (see page 14) are used with a short beam between them. The Forth Railway Bridge in Scotland is one example.

Lifting bridges

Lifting bridges are supported at one end so that they can be raised to let ships pass. Tower Bridge in London is one example.

What to do

Make a lifting bridge like this from corrugated cardboard.

1. Notice that adding a weight (a *counter weight*) fixed high up makes the bridge very easy to raise. This saves energy and might make it possible for just one person raise and lower a bridge.

2. Try different amounts of weight. Can you add too much? What would happen if the arch was taller?

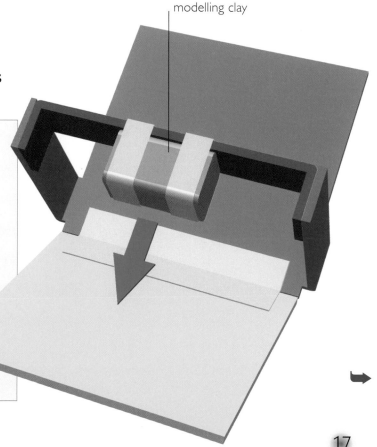

modelling clay

Arch bridges

The Romans found that wedge-shaped stones called *voussoirs* could carry heavy loads when built into an arch. Look out for arches in buildings as well as bridges. Materials that stand up well to compression (squashing), like stone and brick, are used. Modern arches are often made from reinforced concrete. Arches are built over a support that is taken away once the last piece, the middle or keystone, is in place. Strong support is needed at the ends of the arch to stop it spreading outwards.

1

2

keystone

template

20°

thin card support

What to do

1. Lay a thin sheet of card between two heavy books. Gradually add weights to see how much it will carry.

2. Now make the card into an arch and see how much more weight it will take. Is a high arch stronger or weaker than a low one?

To make an arch that will be strong although the pieces are not fixed together:

1. Trace off the template below and use it to make an arch in modelling clay.

2. Cut the arch into the nine voussoirs with a table knife. Build the arch between heavy books on a thin card support.

3. Once the arch is complete, carefully take away the support. Press down gradually to feel how strong an arch can be.

You could go on to try higher and lower arches.

Suspension bridges

Suspension bridges can reach across (or *span*) large distances without using lots of material. In jungle areas they are sometimes made from creepers and bamboo. Suspension bridges carrying roads rely on strong steel cables in tension (being pulled). The pulling forces on one cable are in equilibrium, one force is balanced by another (see page 14). Wind can be a danger to suspension bridges and they have to be designed to cope with it.

deck

tower

base

direction of tubes

What to do

Here is how to make a basic suspension bridge from corrugated cardboard and string. The tubes inside the cardboard must run along the length of each piece.

1. Make the two towers and tape these to a thick cardboard base.

2. Make a deck to reach between the towers.

3. Tie on the strings as shown. Add weight gradually to the centre of your bridge to test it.

Look for ways to improve the basic design. How could you·stiffen the deck? (see page 8.) Would taller towers make the bridge stronger?

Getting ideas

Find out more about bridges by looking in books and perhaps using a CD-ROM. Where are there famous bridges and which is the longest? Make a display about bridges and collect pictures of them. Try to sort them into different kinds e.g. beam, cantilever, arch and suspension bridges. You could add your own bridges and information about your tests. How many stories, songs or poems about bridges can you find? Perhaps you could write some?

Imagine what would happen if all the bridges vanished. Look at and draw or photograph bridges in your area.

Domes
Exploring rounded shapes

Domes were first built long ago and they are found in many countries. They vary in shape when seen from the side but they are all circular when seen from above. Domes have been made from clay, wooden poles thatched with palms, fabric, metal, concrete and even snow. A dome is a kind of shell structure (page 10). A dome can enclose a large space using less material than other structures, and rounded shapes are often stronger than flat ones. If you were to cut a slice from the middle of a dome, you would have made an arch (page 18), which is a strong shape when pressed under weight.

Try making these dome structures to see how strong they can be.

press down

Tip ✓
If you scoop out the inside of half an orange or grapefruit you have also made a dome.

You will need

● plastic bottle
● clear tape
● corrugated cardboard
● round balloon
● newspaper
● flour and water

What to do

1. With adult help, cut the top from a plastic bottle to make a dome.

2. Press down on the top to feel what a strong shape a dome is. Squeeze from the side and the dome feels much weaker.

squeeze

What to do

To make a dome using a balloon as a *former*.

1. Wear an apron and cover your working area with plastic sheet.

2. Cut a circular hole in a piece of corrugated cardboard to hold the balloon.

3. Blow up the balloon so that it fits snugly in the hole and tie the neck. Support the bottom of the balloon in a box or bowl.

4. Mix flour with a little water at a time to make a creamy paste. Tear strips of newspaper about 2cm wide.

4. Brush the strips with the paste, and lay them over the balloon and base. Continue adding strips until you have a layer about 3mm thick.

5. Leave in a warm place to dry well while you work on the ideas below. When dry, pop the balloon and you have a dome!

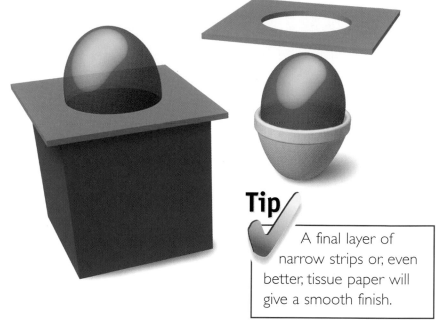

Tip ✓ A final layer of narrow strips or, even better, tissue paper will give a smooth finish.

pastry brush

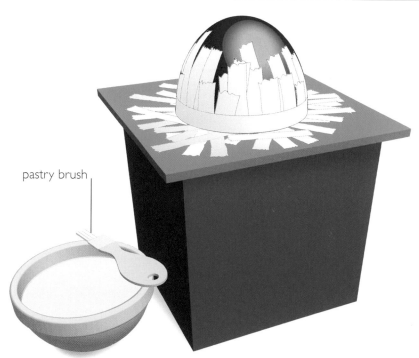

Getting ideas

Your dome could be part of a design for a building of the future or even part of a city or village of the future. You could model the outside of the building and its surroundings and draw what it is like inside. You could go on to model the inside too. What will the building be for? How could you make your building kind to the environment? Where would the building be built? It could be in a desert, under the sea or even on another planet. Look at homes from different times, countries and climates.

Look for domes near where you live or in books and on CD-ROM.

Structures that collapse
Designing structures that fold flat

We can design structures that are strong and rigid but collapse and fold flat when we want them to. This saves a lot of space and makes the products easier to transport. Collapsible structures are all around us; they include folding pushchairs, ironing boards, tent frames and camping or picnic furniture. Blow-up water toys, swimming armbands and even armchairs can be collapsed by letting the air out. Can you think of more things that can be collapsed? Fold-flat furniture would allow a hall or room to be cleared for games or dancing. Lots of flattened shelters could fit into one rescue aircraft. Try out some collapsible structures, think of uses for them and perhaps design your own. Read page 23 for some ideas to help you.

You will need

- corrugated cardboard to make the structures
- brown paper tape or thin card
- thin card or paper

What to do

1. Look at the picture at the bottom. The arrow shows the way the tubes in the corrugated cardboard go. Mark yours out so that the tubes run the same way.

2. Cut out the pieces you need from strips that are about 8cm wide. Mark out the shapes to look like the pictures.

3. Make the creases or joins and put your structures together. To make sharp creases in the right place press down on the line with a ruler and lift the corrugated cardboard to bend it.

4. Press gently on your structures from different directions. Do they feel weaker when pressed some ways compared with others?

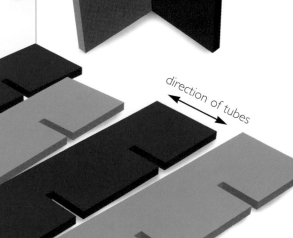

direction of tubes

The slots lock together like this

22

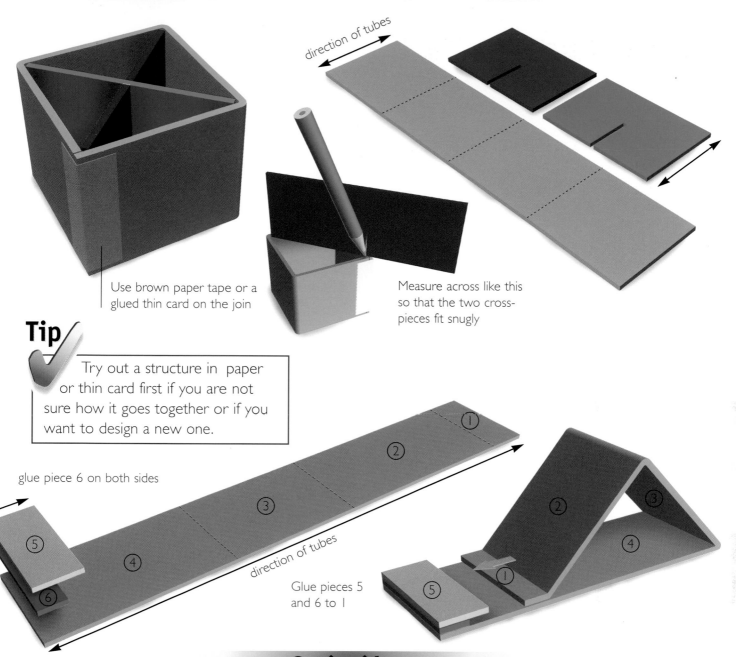

Use brown paper tape or a
glued thin card on the join

Measure across like this
so that the two cross-
pieces fit snugly

Tip Try out a structure in paper
or thin card first if you are not
sure how it goes together or if you
want to design a new one.

direction of tubes

glue piece 6 on both sides

Glue pieces 5
and 6 to 1

direction of tubes

Getting ideas

Look at the structures you have made.
Turn them different ways up. What
could they be used for? Could they
store or hold something? Could you
design a gift that would be easy to post
to someone? Could you design games
that use the structures? What could go
in the holes: pencils, marbles or
something else? You could paint or
decorate your finished object. You
could design a display stand for one
of your favourite things. Look for fold-
flat corrugated cardboard display stands
in shops. Imagine that your structures
were much bigger and perhaps made
from something else. Draw some ideas
for using bigger collapsible structures.
Ideas could include furniture, survival
shelters or something for the beach.
Could you draw fold-flat ideas to help
someone who could not find a spare
seat on a train?

Pop-ups
Structures that seem to vanish!

Some structures can fold flat then almost put *themselves* up. Children's play tents and tunnels can pop up when taken out of their bag. Life rafts are inflated by gas cylinders and some life vests blow up automatically when a person falls in the water. Some greetings cards pop up when they are taken out of their envelope. Pop-ups are often used in books to make things look realistic. They are also used in advertising. Try making these structures that pop up when a folded card is opened.

You will need

● coloured card A4 size
● colouring equipment

What to do

To make each pop-up:

1. Cut a piece of A4 card in half and fold one piece in two to make a base.

2. Draw the *net* of the pop-up carefully on the other piece. Cut the solid lines and score on the dotted ones.

3. Make your pop-ups look like the ones in the pictures. Glue any tabs – don't use too much.

4. Fold the base card and the pop-up should vanish inside.

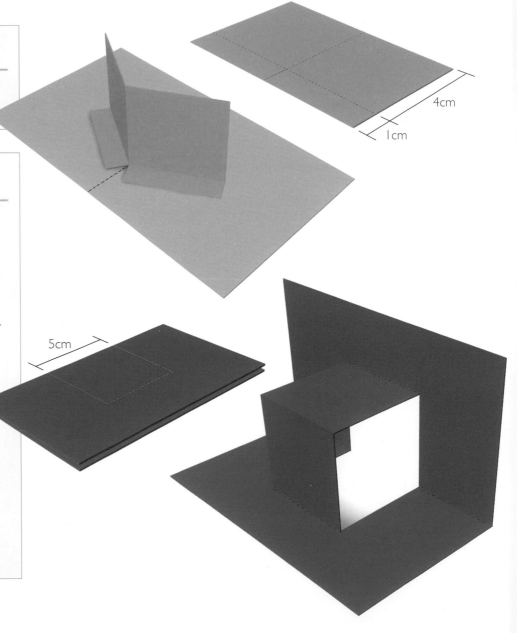

4cm

1cm

5cm

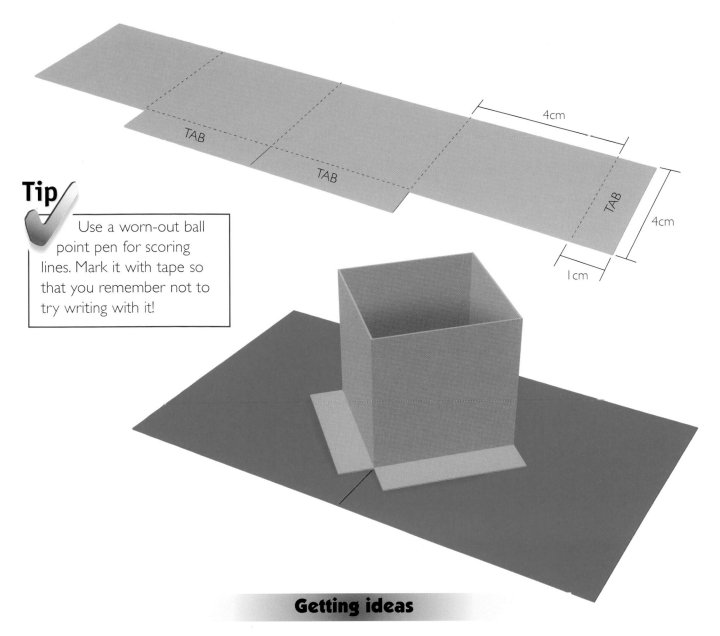

4cm

4cm

1cm

TAB

TAB

TAB

Tip

Use a worn-out ball point pen for scoring lines. Mark it with tape so that you remember not to try writing with it!

Getting ideas

What could you use your pop-ups for? Turn the pop-ups and look at them from different angles to get ideas. You could put more than one pop-up on each folding base. Try making your pop-ups into greetings cards or games. Perhaps you could design a greetings card that is also a game! Could games pieces be thrown into a pop-up, rolled at it or fished out of it? Do holes or slots need to be cut? You also need to think about the age of the user and the kind of rules they could understand.

Use computer word-processing and graphics if you can.

Imagine that your the pop-ups were much bigger and draw your ideas. You would need to use corrugated cardboard if you went on to make big pop-ups. What could large pop-ups be used for? Could the last pop-up (above) be used to make furniture or a play house if it was big enough? Look for examples of pop-up structures and try to see how they work.

Structures that protect
Designing packaging for fragile objects

Natural structures that give protection include seed cases, nuts, crab shells and egg shells. Your skull does the important job of protecting your brain. People make structures to protect our bodies, food and other things. Can you think of things that are packaged to protect them? Protection can be springy like plastic bubble wrap and foam, or rigid like plastic or metal. Protective packaging allows fragile things to be transported or posted without damage. Like other well-designed structures, a good package uses as little material as possible to do the job. This saves weight and money, and is kind to our environment.

See what super structures you can design to protect fragile objects.

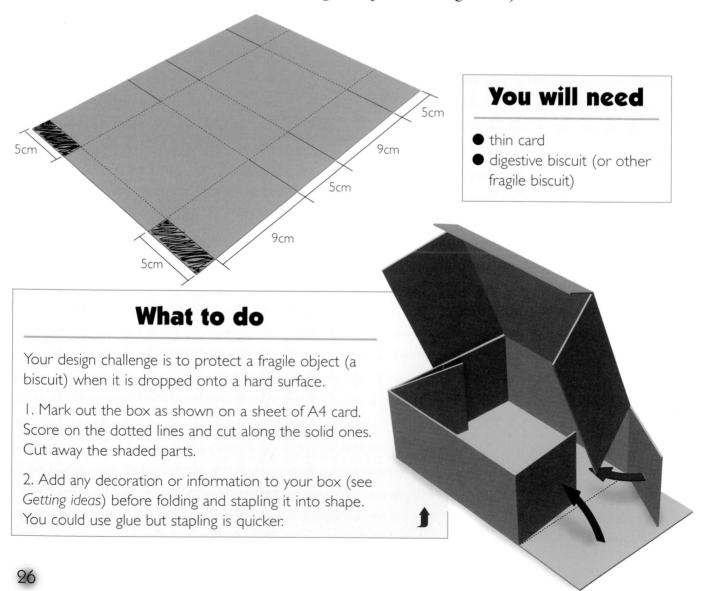

5cm · 5cm · 9cm · 5cm · 9cm · 5cm · 9cm

You will need

- thin card
- digestive biscuit (or other fragile biscuit)

What to do

Your design challenge is to protect a fragile object (a biscuit) when it is dropped onto a hard surface.

1. Mark out the box as shown on a sheet of A4 card. Score on the dotted lines and cut along the solid ones. Cut away the shaded parts.

2. Add any decoration or information to your box (see *Getting ideas*) before folding and stapling it into shape. You could use glue but stapling is quicker.

3. Explore things that could go in your box to protect the biscuit (see pages 6–9). Make your protection ideas and fit them in with the biscuit.

4. Hold the box closed with a little masking tape so that you can open it easily later.

5. Starting quite low, drop the box *bottom down* onto a hard surface like concrete. Drop five times then check for damage. If the biscuit survives, gradually increase the height you drop from.

Safety: you could stand on a chair but for any greater heights you *must* get adult help.

Tip

Remember that broken biscuits are not wasted they can still be eaten or put on a bird table!

shapes that you can try to 'protect' your biscuit with

Getting ideas

Here are some more things to try. You could just draw your ideas or go on to make and try them. Try protecting the biscuit using a range of salvaged materials. Imagine the package is to be delivered by post – keep it as light as you can to keep the price of postage low. Play around with ideas for delivering the biscuit safely. Could a parachute be used, or a slide? Sometimes crazy ideas turn out to be useful. Can you think of other ways to test a package? Could you design something using elastic bands to launch

a package against a wall? How could you measure how much force was being used each time? Cars with dummies inside are crash-tested to see how safe they will be for real people. You could draw or model a car that you think would protect the passengers really well. Collect packaging and look at it closely. Packaging is often used to make people want to buy what is inside as well as protecting it, and it may also give instructions. You could design a package like this to help sell a product that you have made up.

Containers

Resisting forces from inside

Natural containers include eggs, nests, seashells and kangaroos' pouches. People have made containers from many different materials including clay, fabric, glass, wood, card and steel. Containers are used to hold, store, protect and carry all sorts of things. Sacks, nets, cans, buckets and bowls are just a few examples of containers that have to cope with forces from inside.

Thousands of paper bags are used every day to hold and carry things. See if you can design and make a strong, long-lasting, useful and attractive paper bag. Before you make your finished bag, make a *prototype* to try out your ideas.

You will need

- sheet of A3 paper
- materials like card, string and plastic that could be used to make bag handles
- corrugated cardboard to make dividers

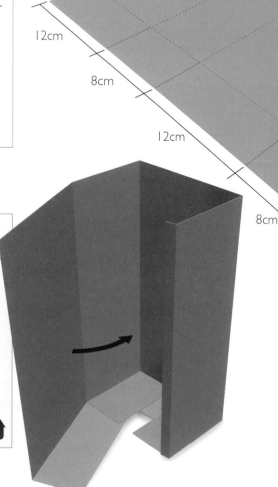

5cm

12cm

8cm

12cm

8cm

crease and fold along dashed lines, cut along the solid lines

What to do

1. Follow the pictures to measure, cut and fold the basic prototype bag. Stick with white glue and leave to dry well.

2. Read the first part of 'getting ideas', then design handles for your bag.

Tip

You could use a stapler as well as glue to fix handles.

28

3. Hang your bag up and gradually load it with weights like oranges or blocks of modelling clay to see how it copes.

You could make more than one bag and try different ideas for handles or compare your ideas with handles made by your friends.

Once you have made a strong prototype bag that is comfortable to carry, you could use what you have learned to make a finished project. Just one person's idea is shown. What will yours be like?

Think about what will go in your bag. Would carton dividers keep the contents in good condition or make them easier to find?

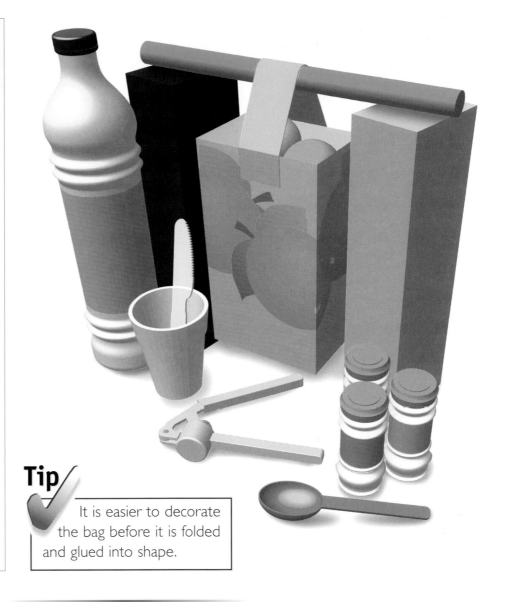

Tip It is easier to decorate the bag before it is folded and glued into shape.

Getting ideas

Bags are used for lots of different things. Handles make bags easier to carry. Look at handles on rucksacks, sports bags, carrier bags and others you can find. What could you use to make bag handles that are strong and comfortable? How will you join them to the bag? Does the bag need to be made stronger where handles are fixed? How could you do this? Can you make other parts of the bag stronger?

What will your bag be used for? You could add dividers to make different layers. Sweet things might be needed last at a picnic and could go on the bottom. Could you make a structure to stop them being squashed? Would pockets make things easier to find? Does the bag need to be kept closed? How could you do this if it did? You could decorate your bag with paints, perhaps by printing with a carved potato (get adult help) or by sticking things on. Can you think of other ways to improving the basic bag design?

Index